Working for our Future

Fighting Disease

Judith Anderson with Christian Aid

SEA-TO-SEA

Mankato Collingwood London

This edition first published in 2010 by
Sea-to-Sea Publications
Distributed by Black Rabbit Books
P.O. Box 3263, Mankato, Minnesota 56002

Printed in USA

Library of Congress Cataloging-in-Publication Data

Anderson, Judith (Judith Mary)
  Fighting disease / Judith Anderson with Christian Aid.
     p. cm. -- (Working for our future)
  Includes index.
  ISBN 978-1-59771-194-4 (hardcover)
 1. Communicable diseases--Juvenile literature. 2. Charities--Juvenile literature. I. Christian Aid. II. Title.
  RC112.A623 2010
  362.196'9--dc22

                              2008044884

9 8 7 6 5 4 3 2

Published by arrangement with the Watts Publishing Group Ltd., London.

Editor: Jeremy Smith
Art director: Jonathan Hair
Design: Rita Storey

Produced in association with Christian Aid. Franklin Watts would like to thank Christian Aid for their help with this title, in particular for allowing permission to use the information concerning Maria and Marbella and Josué and Jaeli which is © Christian Aid. We would also like to thank the parents of Atkmatbek for the information and photographs provided.

Picture credits: Adrian Arbib/Christian Aid: 3br, 10l, 13t, 16b, 24b. Alamy: 1, 4b, 6t, 10t, 11b, 13b, 25. Annabel Davis/Christian Aid: 3bc, 6b, 7, 12t, 20-21 all. Eduardo Martino/Christian Aid: 3bl, 8-9 all, 15b, 19b, 23t. istockphoto.com: 27b.

The Millennium Development Goals

In 2000, government leaders agreed on eight goals to help build a better, fairer world in the 21st century. These goals include getting rid of extreme poverty, fighting child mortality and disease, promoting education, gender equality, and maternal health, and ensuring sustainable development.

The aim of this series is to look at the problems these goals address, show how they are being tackled at local level, and relate them to the experiences of children around the world.

Contents

The Cast

Follow the stories of these five children from around the world, all affected by disease in different ways.

Atkmatbek is 10 years old. He lives in Kyrgyzstan in Central Asia with his father and mother.

Dolly Akter is 16 years old. She lives in Dhaka, the capital of Bangaladesh.

Marbella is 7 years old. She lives with her mother, **Maria**, in Honduras, Central America. She likes riding her bicycle.

Josué (right), age 7, and **Jaeli (left),** age 5, live in Angola with their mother. They like to help her bake cakes.

Good health

Do you feel well? Do you have lots of energy? Do you eat nutritious food, get a good night's sleep, and get plenty of exercise? If you can answer yes to these questions, then you are probably very healthy. That's great!

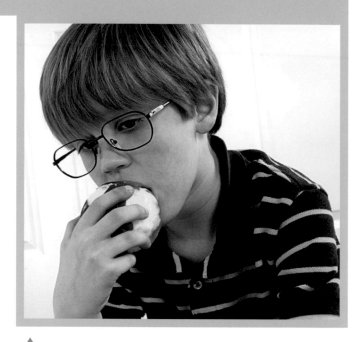

Plenty of fresh fruit and vegetables helps children grow strong and stay healthy. It gives them energy and helps them fight off illness.

Feeling sick

Good health is something we don't often think about until we feel sick. However, most of us suffer from colds, coughs, or an upset stomach at some point. These common infections spread easily from person to person, making us feel unwell. We may lose our appetite, or have less energy for a day or two. Then we recover.

❝ When I had a bad cold I had to miss my friend's birthday party. **❞**

Kelli, age 10

A common cold can spread quickly from person to person.

Getting better

If you are normally quite healthy, your body can fight off a mild illness by itself. If the illness is more severe—flu perhaps, or an asthma attack or a bad stomach bug—then your doctor may give you some medicine to help you get better. Fortunately, many of us live within traveling distance of a clinic or a hospital where we can get treatment whenever we need it. Most people in the developed world take good health and good health care for granted, but not everyone around the world can do this.

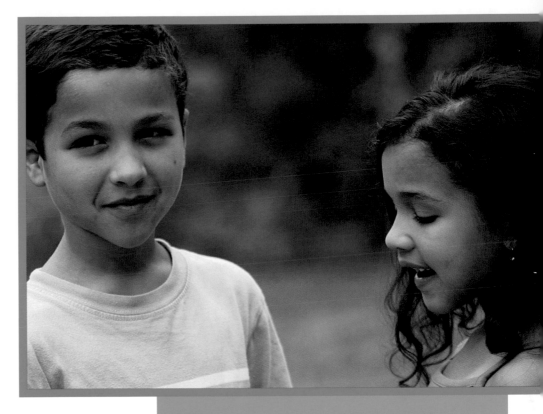

Raul, age 8

"Last year nearly half the children in my class were sick at the same time. It was the flu. My teacher was sick too. Then we got better."

Medicines for many common illnesses can be bought over the counter at a pharmacy or drugstore.

? **What is the best thing about being healthy? Why is it important to eat well if you want to stay healthy?**

No health care?

Some people do not have access to doctors, nurses, clinics, or medicines. This may be because they cannot afford them, or it may be because there are no facilities where they live. If no one is sick, this isn't a problem. But what if someone is seriously ill? They might spread the illness to other people. They might die if they don't get treatment.

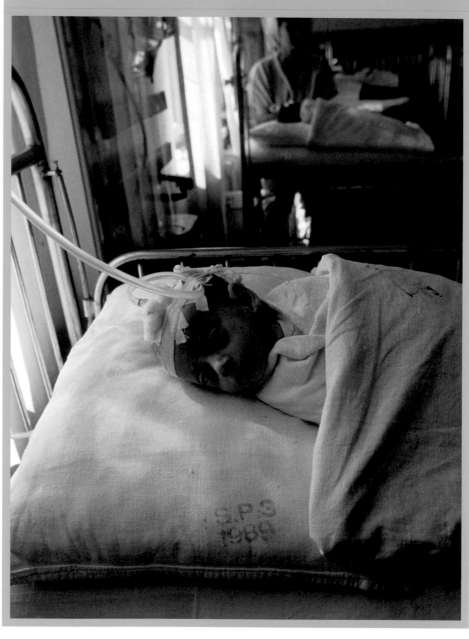

Common illnesses

Have you ever had an upset stomach? Vomiting and diarrhea are unpleasant, but it is extremely rare for someone who is usually healthy and well fed to die from their effects. However, when someone is already weak from lack of food or water, such infections quickly become life threatening. In less developed countries with a shortage of basic medical care, diarrhea kills millions of children every year.

 This child is suffering from diarrhea and malnutrition in the Intensive Care Unit at Tirana Childrens Hospital, Albania. Children are especially at risk from diarrhea because they are not as strong as adults. Losing a lot of body fluid can be very dangerous for a child.

6

Immunization

When you were a baby, you were probably given an injection or a drop on the tongue to protect you against various common diseases. This is known as immunization. It means our bodies become immune to a particular type of infection. Not all disease can be prevented by immunization, but some diseases have completely disappeared because of it, while other diseases, such as polio and measles, are much less common now. However, many people in less developed countries are not immunized. They continue to suffer from diseases that we know can be prevented.

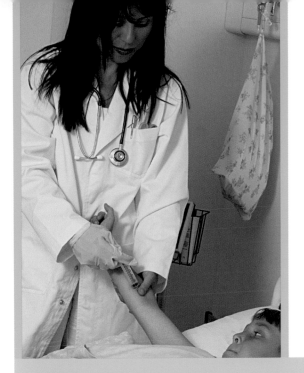

❝ A child can be immunized for $30. It is one of the simplest, most efficient, most cost-effective ways of improving living standards on our planet. **❞**

Statistic from the Global Alliance for Vaccines and Information.

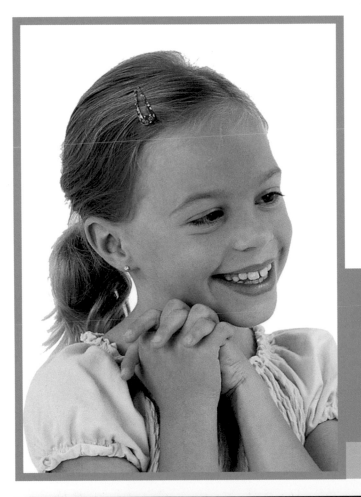

❝ I've been immunized against tuberculosis. I had the injection when I was a baby. I can't remember it but I'm glad I've had it! **❞**

Marianne, age 9.

? **Have you been immunized against any diseases? If so, which ones?**

The problem of disease

An infectious disease is an illness that spreads from person to person. Not all disease is infectious. Heart disease, for example, cannot be caught from someone else. The problem with infectious diseases is that they can spread very quickly through the population, often with devastating results.

The spread of disease

People catch diseases in different ways. Some diseases, such as the flu and tuberculosis, are spread by infected people coughing and sneezing. Diarrhea is spread by drinking unclean food or water or contact with sewage because of poor sanitation. A serious disease called malaria is spread by a certain type of mosquito.

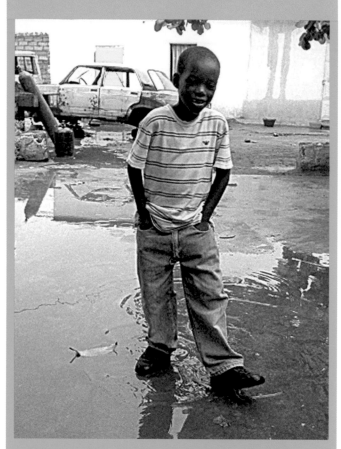

❝ Malaria comes when a mosquito bites you and then bad stuff from the mosquito gets inside you and then you're sick. **❞**

Josué and his younger sister Jaeli live with their mother in Luanda, the capital city of Angola. Mosquitoes breed in the pools of stagnant water that collect in the streets after it rains. Recently, both children became very sick with malaria.

Not all mosquitoes spread malaria. The malarial mosquito (left) is found in hot countries and is mainly active at night.

Akhmatbek lives in a town called Bishek in Kyrgyzstan with his mother and father. Four months ago his father became very ill with tuberculosis.

" We didn't know what was wrong with him. He couldn't go to work and then he lost his job. He was very weak and couldn't get out of bed. He had a very bad cough. **"**

Around the world

Different diseases affect some parts of the world more than others. Diarrhea is a particularly severe problem in countries where basic sanitation and clean water are hard to come by. Malaria affects people in hot countries where a particular type of mosquito is common. Tuberculosis is found all over the world, but affects poorer people most because they don't have access to a good diet and medicines to help them fight the disease.

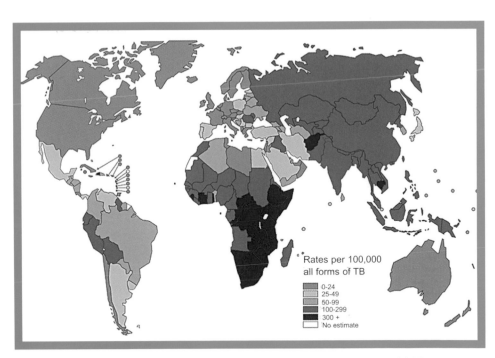

Rates per 100,000 all forms of TB

- 0-24
- 25-49
- 50-99
- 100-299
- 300 +
- No estimate

▲ A map showing the number of deaths from tuberculosis in 2003.

? Akhmatbek lives in a single room with his parents. What do you think are his chances of becoming infected with tuberculosis?

HIV/AIDS

You have probably heard of a disease called HIV/AIDS. At the moment there is no cure for this disease. Certain drugs help delay the symptoms but they are very expensive. Another problem with HIV/AIDS is that many people do not know they are infected ntil after they have passed it on to others.

Estimated Number of AIDS-Related Deaths Worldwide, 1980–2000

Source: UNAIDS

 A graph showing the rise in the number of deaths from AIDS between 1980–2000.

An estimated 15 million children around the world have lost one or both parents to HIV/AIDS. These children are in an orphanage in Ukraine. Their parents died of HIV/AIDS.

What is HIV/AIDS?

AIDS is a disease caused by a virus called HIV. HIV is spread through infected blood (during a blood transfusion or an injection using a dirty needle) or by having unprotected sex. People may have HIV without knowing about it at first. However, when the disease takes hold, their immune system (the body's natural defense against illness) breaks down and they are no longer healthy enough to fight off other illnesses. This is why many HIV/AIDS sufferers actually die of diseases such as tuberculosis and pneumonia, which would be unlikely to kill somebody without the virus.

The effects on families

HIV/AIDS is particularly devastating to families, because the infection often passes between both parents, and can also pass from an expectant mother to her unborn child. The disease continues to grow steadily all around the world, creating families in which both parents have died and orphaned children have become the main carers for their young and often sick siblings.

" We found out that Marbella was infected when she was five years old. **"**

Maria Dolores talks about when she was told her daughter Marbella had the HIV virus. She was probably passed it by her mother before she was born.

? **How do you think Marbella's mother felt when she found out that Marbella has HIV?**

How does disease affect people?

If a serious infectious disease is left untreated, the infected person may die. Not only this, but they may spread the disease to other people while they are still alive. There are many other consequences, too. A sick person cannot work or look after their family. They may have to rely on their children to care for them.

" When I found out that I was infected with HIV I felt as though the world had ended. I thought I was going to die soon and that I was going to leave my children as orphans. **"**

Marbella's mother Maria describes the terrible moment when she discovered she had the HIV virus.

Families

Because infectious disease spreads from person to person, whole families can become ill very quickly. When this happens, parents may be too unwell to look after sick children. Without a family member old enough or well enough to fetch water, prepare food, buy medicine, look after the farm, or go to school, the future soon begins to look very bleak.

A chart from 2005 showing global deaths from four major diseases. ▶

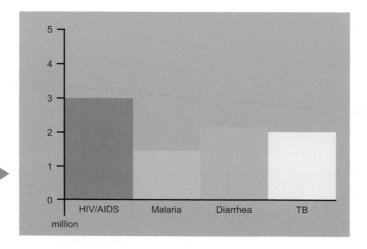

The cycle of poverty and disease

One of the biggest problems of disease is the poverty it creates. When someone is ill, they cannot work. They cannot grow food or earn a wage. They may become homeless, or they may find they cannot afford to eat properly or buy medicine. This means they are less likely to get better. They become trapped in a cycle of poverty and disease.

Akhmatbek's father did not get the treatment he needed in the poorly equipped hospital in his country.

When Akhmatbek's father became ill with tuberculosis, he lost his job and the family couldn't afford to eat properly.

" Mom said that Dad needed soup. But we only had bread and tea. **"**

? **What would help break the cycle of poverty and disease in Akhmatbek's family?**

Why are so many people affected?

Many infectious diseases are either preventable, or curable. Yet in Africa, a child dies of malaria every ten seconds. Around the world, someone dies of tuberculosis every 15 seconds, and more than 40 million people worldwide are now infected with HIV/AIDS. Why?

Poverty

One of the main reasons for the continued growth in infectious disease is poverty. Poverty means people cannot afford to eat well and have access to good sanitation and clean water. Poverty means people cannot afford immunizations, medicines, and doctors' fees. Poverty means people live in cramped and overcrowded housing where disease spreads even faster.

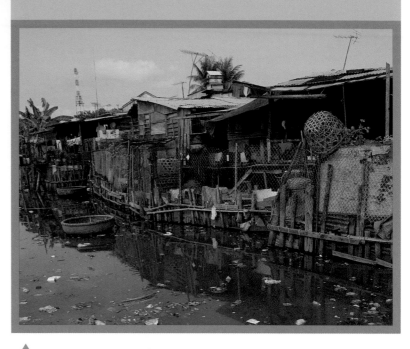

▲ A typical slum in Dhaka, Bangladesh, with open, dirty water flowing through. One in six of the world's population have to drink unsafe water every day.

Bill Gates, Chairman of Microsoft and the Bill Gates Foundation, which give donations to help poorer countries fight disease.

" Millions of children have died from malaria because they were not protected by an insecticide-treated bed net or did not receive effective treatment. We can stop this tragedy. "

Lack of information

Nevertheless, some methods of preventing the spread of disease are cheap and simple. An inexpensive mosquito net over a child's bed at night will protect them from malaria, while information on basic hygiene can stop the spread of diseases such as diarrhea and tuberculosis. But how do people in remote or poorer areas receive this information? Teachers have to be trained and paid for. It all comes back to money.

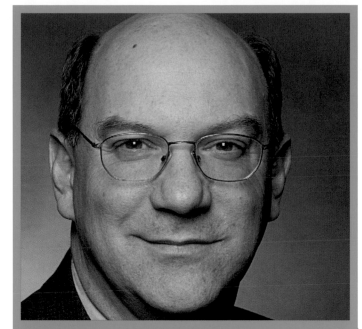

" South Africa's Malaria Control Program has been quite successful in establishing procedures for mosquito control; looking to educate people in at-risk areas. "

Eugene Brantly, Malaria Progam Director at a research institute called RTI International, speaks about the success of its education program in South Africa. It delivers malaria prevention and treatment messages to more than 600,000 South Africans.

An Indian poster from 2006 instructing people how stop malaria from spreading.

What would you do to make sure that everyone learns how to prevent the spread of diseases like malaria?

The Millennium Development Goals

Many diseases are preventable, yet because of poverty and lack of education millions of people continue to be infected every year. In the year 2000, the world's leaders met and agreed a set of eight goals that would help to make the world a better, fairer place in the 21st century. All eight goals are connected and in order to achieve them, every single country, rich and poor, needs to work together and play a part.

French President Chirac (right) welcomes UN Secretary-General Kofi Annan and British Prime Minister Blair at the Élysée Palace to discuss the Millennium Development Goals in 2003.

The Goals

All eight goals have targets that need to be reached by the year 2015, and governments have been asked to make policies to ensure these targets are met. The target for fighting disease is to stop the spread of malaria, tuberculosis, and HIV/AIDS by 2015. This can only be achieved through the success of prevention programs as well as treatment programs. It requires a huge commitment from every single country in the world.

1 Get rid of extreme poverty and hunger

2 Primary education for all

3 Promote equal chances for girls and women

4 Reduce child mortality

5 Improve the health of mothers

6 Combat HIV/AIDS, malaria, and other diseases

7 Ensure environmental sustainability

8 Address the special needs of developing countries, including debt and fair trade

MILLENNIUM CAMPAIGN

A spokesperson for the Millennium Campaign (logo shown left).

▲ **A poster educating the public about AIDS in Hanoi, Vietnam.**

" We need everyone's voice to join together and demand that governments live up to their promises to achieve the Millennium Development Goals by 2015. **"**

A global concern

The problem of HIV/AIDS and other diseases is not just a concern for countries in the developing world. Under the commitments made in the Millennium Development Goals, world leaders agreed to push drugs companies to make vaccines and treatments for deadly diseases available to everyone in the world—not just those people who can afford them. With people moving from developing countries to other places, it is also vital to help these people stay disease free in order to stop such illnesses spreading further across the globe.

A leaflet about HIV/AIDS in Zambia says:

" It's my problem.

It's your problem.

It's our problem.

So what are you going to do about it? **"**

? **Leaflets like the one on HIV/AIDS help raise awareness about disease. But many people in developing countries cannot read. How can these people be given the information they need?**

Government action

Disease is a global problem. It has the potential to affect every single one of us. So halting and reversing the spread of the most serious infectious diseases requires a global response. All countries and governments need to work together to bring about change and ensure a healthier world.

 A young child receiving a vaccination for polio in Addis-Ababa, Ethiopia.

 A poorly facilitated hospital in Lagos, Nigeria.

What governments can do

Governments of poorer, less economically developed countries can put people first by training more doctors and nurses, building more clinics and hospitals, and providing medicines and immunization programs. They can also teach people how to prevent disease through simple measures, such as better hygiene.

18

Sharing the cost

Governments of richer, more economically developed countries can provide financial help so more health services are available to poorer people who are often at most risk from disease. They can invest in research to develop new medicines and immunizations. They can also reduce the cost of expensive drugs and equipment that poorer countries need and make sure these treatments are readily available.

▲ A vaccine for tuberculosis is tested in a Swiss laboratory. Making this vaccnine affordable for people in poorer countries drastically cuts the death rate from the disease.

Success stories

Some global responses are already having an effect. The World Health Organization has developed a special program known as DOTS to help combat tuberculosis. In countries that have committed themselves to this program, the number of cases being detected and then cured has risen sharply.

This mother from Afghanistan had tuberculosis. She is now better and able to look after her family because of the joint efforts of the World Health Organization and the World Food Program, which gave her the medicines she needed. ▶

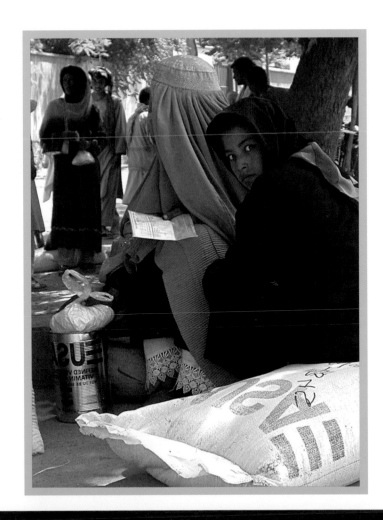

? **Why is it so important that all countries work together to stop the spread of disease?**

Local solutions

Governments must work together to make new policies and provide more money in the fight against disease. However, much of the vital work of immunizing children and running clinics and health education programs is carried out by charities and aid organizations who can respond quickly to the needs of local communities.

Fighting tuberculosis in Kyrgyzstan

Akhmatbet's father was very ill at first, but because he lost his job he could not afford to stay in the hospital. Then a nurse from the local branch of the Red Crescent Society began to visit him at home every day. She made sure he received the medicine he needed, checked on his progress and even brought food for the family. Now he is well enough to go to the Red Crescent canteen each day where he is given his medicine and a hot meal. Nurse Svetlana Sooronova of the Kyrgyz Red Crescent Society says that many of the people she treats do not have the money to get to a hospital or doctor, and are rejected by their relatives for fear of infection. She says these people rely totally on the Red Crescent Society.

❝ I like the nurses. They made my father better and now he plays chess with me again. ❞

Akhmatbek

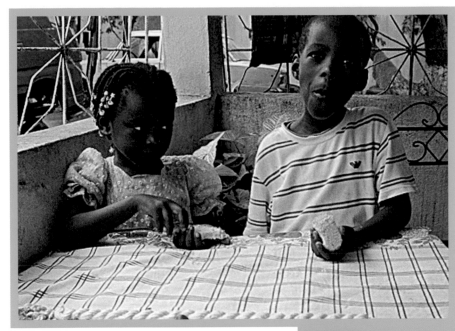

Jaeli (far left) and Josué (quoted below) were nursed back to health by their mother, Tabita (below).

"We were sick, I was hot. Mommy looked after me and gave me medicine. Then I was better.**"**

Combating sickness in Angola

In Angola, the Evangelical Congregational Church (IECA) runs a project to teach poorer women about health and hygiene. The project is based in Luanda, the capital city, where malaria and diarrhea are very common. The IECA taught Josué and Jaeli's mother Tabita how to treat various types of sickness. This meant that when her children became ill, she knew what to do.

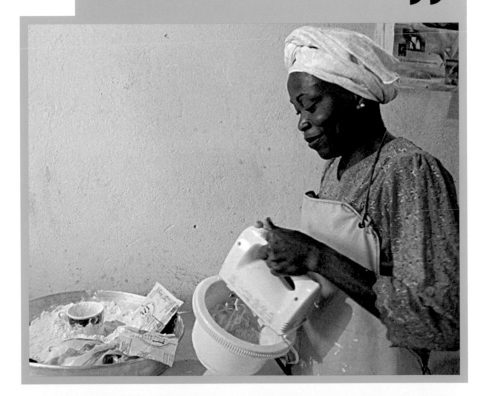

? ▪ **What do you think might have happened to Akhmatbek's father if he had not been visited by a nurse from the Red Crescent Society?**

People who help

People from all over the world are helping fight disease. Doctors, nurses, and teachers travel to local communities to set up clinics, immunize children, and provide information about how to stay healthy. Scientists work to develop new and better medicines, while fundraisers work to raise money for projects such as improving a water supply.

Miss Girja, a worker for the Tamil Nadu Voluntary Health Association (logo above), describes her reasons for wanting to join the organization.

" I was keen to work directly with the community and felt that being a counselor would enable me to have this contact. I am often inspired by the determination and calm manner in which some of the patients I counsel deal with their illnesses. "

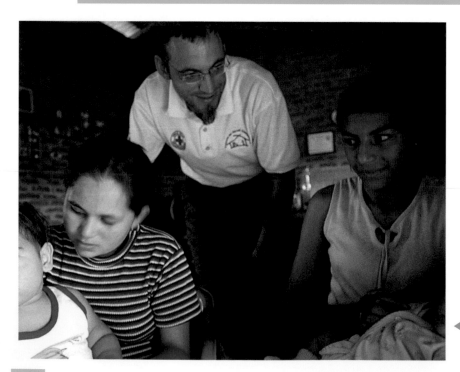

Inspired by others

Counselors are people trained to offer support and advice to those suffering from diseases such as tuberculosis and HIV/AIDS. Miss Girja trained as a counselor for Tamil Nadu Voluntary Health Association in India. Canadian Red Cross worker Richard McCabe helps to provide health promotion, education, and prevention advice.

◀ Canadian Red Cross worker Richard McCabe visits families with health problems in Nicaragua.

Spreading the word

Francisco, age 18, and Nelson, age 16, live in Angola. They have both been specially trained to teach students at their school about how to prevent the spread of HIV/AIDS and malaria.

Nelson (right)

❝ We tell people how the diseases are transmitted and explain how you can avoid getting sick. We need to do this so that people know how to stay healthy. I've had malaria, and so have other people in my family but thankfully we all got better. ❞

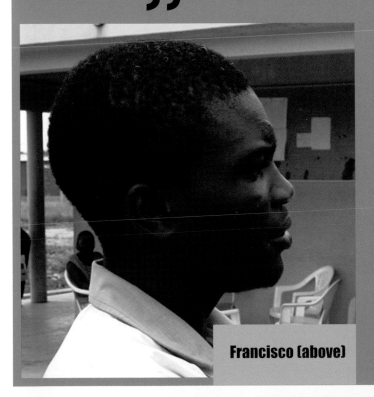

Francisco (above)

❝ We do workshops at school and in the community. For example, we tell them that stagnant water is a breeding ground for mosquitoes, and we show people how to kill mosquitoes with insect spray. It's a very good thing to be involved in. Everybody needs to know about malaria and HIV/AIDS, because lots of people get sick and die from these diseases. ❞

? Why are Francisco and Nelson so keen to help prevent the spread of HIV/AIDS and malaria?

23

Protecting each other

One of the most effective ways of fighting disease is to prevent people from getting sick in the first place. Malaria can be avoided if people learn to take precautions to protect themselves and their families. Tuberculosis can be prevented through immunization. Diarrhea can be reduced if people have access to clean water and teach each other about better hygiene.

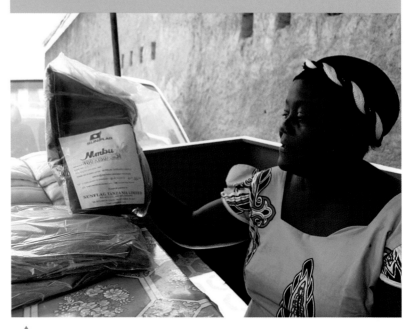

▲ This lady in Angola has set up a stall outside a maternity hospital. She hands out free mosquito nets to expectant mothers, because babies are at extra risk from malaria.

No more malaria

Mosquitoes that carry the malaria infection are mainly active at night. The best way for people to protect each other is to use devices that stop the mosquitoes from reaching you in the first place. Sleeping under a mosquito net or spraying a room with insecticide are cheap, effective ways of reducing the threat. Local groups in centers such as Angola are putting these measures into practice.

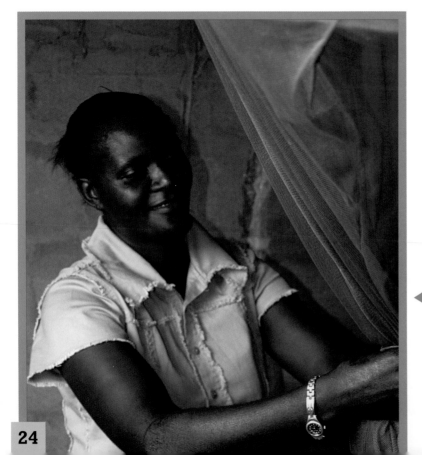

◄ Emilia Nakaué is the head of a small group of volunteers in Angola who had training in malaria and HIV awareness. Since Emilia found out about mosquito nets (shown right of picture), everyone sleeps under them, and none of her three younger children have had the disease.

Reducing diarrhea

Dolly Akter, age 16, lives in a slum neighborhood of Dhaka, the capital of Bangladesh. She is involved in a UNICEF project to improve sanitation and hygiene in her area. She and her friends go from house to house, making sure that people understand the importance of washing and using only clean, covered water.

> **❝** Before it was such a dirty and undeveloped area. Nowadays it is different. The children in our area don't get diarrhea so often, and they laugh and play more now that they are healthier. **❞**

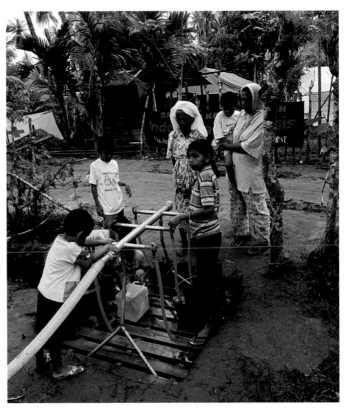

▲ **A water sanitation system set up by French firefighters provides clean water for all the residents of this camp in Indonesia.**

Dolly Akter talks about the changes in her neighborhood in Bangladesh.

? **Dolly visits her neighbors to tell them about good hygiene. What else can be done to reduce the spread of diarrhea in slum areas?**

A brighter future

Fighting disease means many different things. It means preventing the spread of disease by taking protective measures. It means developing better medicines and treating those who are already suffering from disease. It also means fighting one of the principal causes of disease—poverty—so that everyone has a chance of a brighter, healthier future.

Building hope

When Maria Dolores discovered that she and her daughter Marbella were infected with HIV, she didn't know what to do. Their health suffered and she lost all hope. Then she found out about an association of self-help groups for people with HIV/AIDS. She started to attend workshops to learn about her illness and how she could help herself and Marbella. Now she runs a group of her own.

Maria speaks about the work of the group. Everyone helps everybody else out.

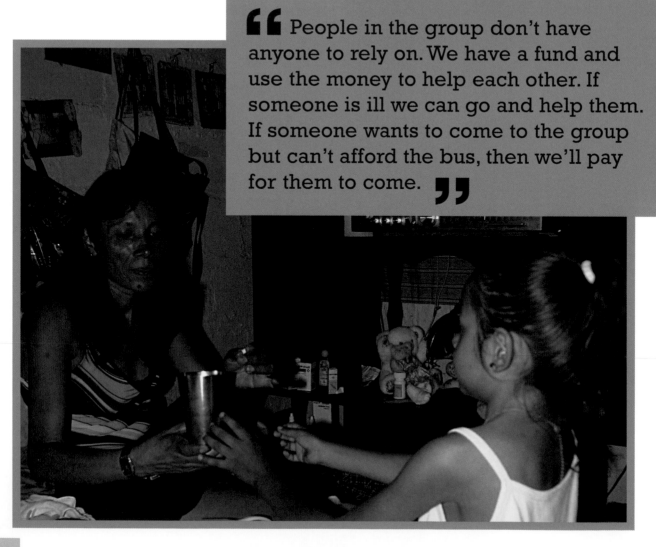

" People in the group don't have anyone to rely on. We have a fund and use the money to help each other. If someone is ill we can go and help them. If someone wants to come to the group but can't afford the bus, then we'll pay for them to come. "

Happy and well

When Josué and Jaeli's mom Tabita went to classes at the IECA center, she didn't only learn about how to prevent and treat malaria. She also learned to cook! Now she supports the family by baking cakes and selling them. She can afford to send Josué and Jaeli to school.

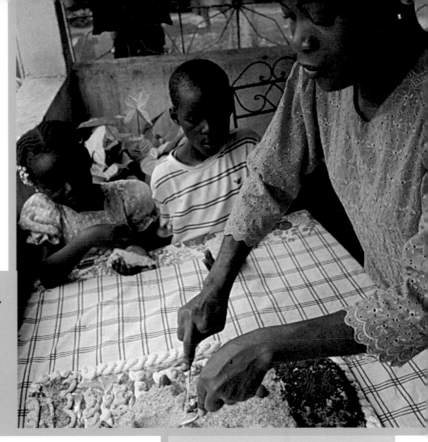

> **❝** I mix the eggs and the cake in the bowl. I like eating the cakes. I like the Christmas tree cake best! **❞**

Tabita describes how she enjoys cooking for her family, especially treats such as cakes.

Dolly Akhter's parents are very clear about the advantages of her training in health and hygiene.

> **❝** Dolly learns more, then our family learns more. We don't get diarrhea any more. Our family always knows about hygiene and being clean, so we don't get sick. **❞**

? **How has educating people like Dolly helped other members of her community?**

Action you can take

Disease causes terrible suffering, prevents people from working, and hinders the development of whole countries. It keeps families in poverty and stops children from getting the education they need. Yet if everyone works together, the spread of disease can be halted and even reversed.

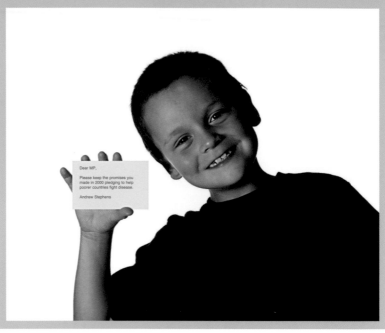

Dear MP,

Please keep the promises you made in 2000 pledging to help poorer countries fight disease.

Andrew Stephens

▲ Write a postcard to the leader of your country demanding that they keep the promises made in the Millennium Development Goals.

▼ Make sure you wash your hands after going to the bathroom to avoid spreading germs.

Write to your government
The problem of disease is greatest in developing countries. Yet there are many things we can do to help those who may seem far away. Campaign for change by writing to your government representative and asking them to uphold the promises enshrined in the Millennium Development Goals.

Take care of yourself
Fighting the spread of disease is the responsibility of every single one of us. The first thing we can do is make sure that we are not spreading disease ourselves. Washing hands, using clean water, eating healthy food, and getting immunized against diseases such as tuberculosis, polio, and measles help us stay healthy. They also mean that we are not putting those around us at risk.

Hold an awareness assembly

Research a particular problem such as diarrhea in a remote village without access to clean water. Then hold an assembly at your school, using words, pictures, and perhaps a short play to raise awareness about the issues.

Join an action group

There are hundreds of charities and action groups that raise money for medicines, equipment, and clinics in the developing world. Many have special youth programs or posters or websites to raise awareness and tell you about specific things you can do to help. Check out charities such as Save the Children, UNICEF, The International Red Crescent and Red Cross, WaterAid, and Health Unlimited. Or set up one of your own!

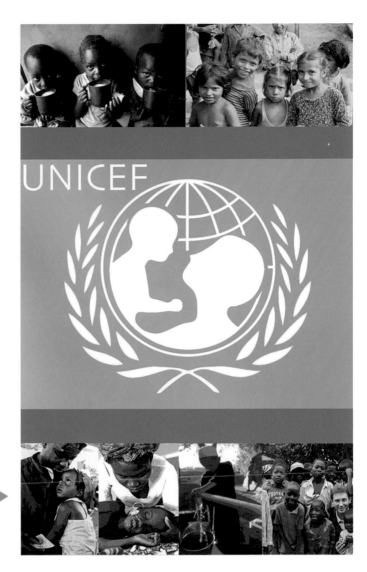

Join a charity or action group such as UNICEF (right).

Raise money

Hold a bake sale, do a sponsored run or swim, offer a hair braiding or shoe shining service, wash cars, or put on a play or concert. There are so many ways to raise money for your chosen charity—the more inventive, the better!

Think of a way to raise money for a charity, such as doing a sponsored swim.

? How will you help to improve the lives of children like Atkmatbek, Dolly, Marbella, Josué, and Jaeli?

Glossary

Charity an organization that uses money donated by members of the public to help others

Diarrhea an illness spread by dirty food and water or not washing hands after going to the bathroom

HIV/AIDS a disease that attacks the body's natural immune system

Hygiene keeping clean

Immunization an injection or medicine that protects us from a particular disease

Infection an illness or disease that we pick up from our environment

Insecticide chemicals that kill insects, such as mosquitoes

Malaria a dangerous disease spread by a type of mosquito that lives in hot, humid climates

Measles a common childhood illness; it kills many children each year in countries that do not immunize against it

Millennium Development Goals (MDGs) eight goals agreed by world leaders in the year 2000 with the aim of eradicating poverty and disease and promoting the rights of disadvantaged people

Mortality death

Nutritious healthy food, good for growth and energy

Polio a disease that affects the spinal cord; immunization programs mean that polio has completely disappeared from many parts of the world

Sanitation drains for dirty water and waste from toilets

Stagnant water water that is no longer fresh; dirty water

Tuberculosis a serious lung infection

United Nations an organization of countries from all around the world with the aim of promoting peace, development, and human rights

Virus a type of disease that spreads from one person to another

Find out more

Useful websites

www.cyberschoolbus.un.org/mdgs
This site introduces all eight Millennium Development Goals with facts, photos, and video clips to illustrate each one.

Send your story or poem about how any of the issues in this book have affected you to: **addyourvoice@un.org** and view stories from other children on the link above (go to "Add your voice").

www.millenniumcampaign.org/goals
The official site for the latest news on the Millennium Development Goals. Click on "Goal 6" to find the latest developments, facts, and statistics as well as information about what you can do in the fight against diseases such as malaria and HIV/AIDS.

www.wateraid.org/usa/
WaterAid works in 17 countries providing water, sanitation, and hygiene education to some of the world's poorest people. Click on "Learn Zone", then "Games" for some great interactive games that allow you to play a role in solving some of the world's water problems. You can also click on "Splash out" to find out about brand new fundraising activities and learn how you can get involved.

www.kidshealth.org/kid/ health_problems/infection/hiv.html
A website all about HIV/AIDS—what it is and how it affects people.

www.ifrc.org
Official website of the Red Cross/Red Crescent organization.

Note to parents and teachers:
Every effort has been made by the Publishers to ensure that these websites are suitable for children, that they are of the highest educational value, and that they contain no inappropriate or offensive material. However, because of the nature of the Internet, it is impossible to guarantee that the contents of these sites will not be altered. We strongly advise that Internet access be supervised by a responsible adult.

Christian Aid websites

Christian Aid contributed two of the real-life stories in this book (the accounts of Josué and Jaeli, and Marbella and Maria). You can find out more about this organization by following the links below:

www.christian-aid.org.uk
The main site for the charity Christian Aid, which helps disadvantaged children and adults all over the world, regardless of their religion.

Index